AF369369

Welcome To Your Life

Poems By

Tony Tracy

Acknowledgments

These poems were written over a 12 year period that was inclusive of many family travels and personal metamorphoses. I want to give a deep heartfelt thanks and appreciation to Dave Wolf, good friend and mentor, who helped me through the revision processes with keen insight and interrogation of many of these poems in their earlier (and later) versions. And finally kudos to the editors of the following journals and magazines where these poems first appeared, often with different titles, content and format. *Bluestem*: "Suicide Psalm"; *Burningwood 90*: "Pops, Dis Playa Need Ta Roll" *Clockhouse*: "The Suburbanite Speaks"; *Coe Review*: "Replacements "*Concho River Review*: Replacements"; *Flint Hills Review*: " Land of Bizarro," "Hailstones*"; Free Lunch*: "Eating Hailstones" *Hotel Amerika*: " The Suburnanite Speaks"; *I-70 Review*:"Dirty Sweet"; *Jelly Bucket*: "The Suburbanite Speaks"; *Janus Head*: "Starring Role"; "Our House"; *New Madrid*: "Physiography"; "The Mirror"; "Suicide Pslam"; *Painted Bride's Quarterly*: "The Stuff of Legend"; *Poet Lore*: "Whore"; *Potomac Review*: " On the Other Side of the Monongahela River"; *Slipsteam*: "Beneath the Bleacher's Din"; *Southern Indiana Review*; "Beneath The Bleacher's Din"; *Poetry East*: "In Training"; *Tar River Poetry*: "Dirty Sweet"; "Eclipse with Reference to Albert Pujols"; "In Training"; Lescarpolette"; "Physiography".

Meta

O' to summon poems like The Greats, to write
        with the same aplomb and measurable grace—
musical gems *even* the old guard couldn't deny;
        phonetics of Marlowe and Dunne, metered pace

of Shakespeare beset with wounded hearts.
        A language built to sound sweet on the ear.
What was the calling card of the avant-garde.
        Though gentlemen and scholars cringed, couldn't bear

the frank, ribald references to sex: *to unpin*
        that spangled breastplate a literary travesty,
" façade of metaphysics" to fend the critic's
        charge of smut. Work that "reveled in God's lucanae".

But when epic skill abounds, who cares. Like dope
mainlined, a serum to give the lovesick hope.

Copyright© 2020 Tony Tracy

ISBN: 978-93-90202-63-8

First Edition: 2020

Rs. 200/-

Cyberwit.net

HIG 45 Kaushambi Kunj, Kalindipuram

Allahabad - 211011 (U.P.) India

http://www.cyberwit.net

Tel: +(91) 9415091004

E-mail: info@cyberwit.net

No part of this book may be reproduced or transmitted in any form or by any means, electronic, mechanical, photocopying, or otherwise, without the express written consent of Tony Tracy.

Printed at Repro India Limited.

Table of Contents

Sonnets & Bref Doubles

Part 3: Departure

Part 1: Early Evidence

The Suburbanite Speaks

The old Hanns-G monitor from Walmart retired years ago, put-
out-to-pasture, shoved to the back-end of the study's table
where it's become a monolith stuck with memos written to the
ubiquitous self — orange and yellow Post-It notes curling
around its empty dust-face to rescue, resuscitate the individual
on mornings when he's overridden by the head's committee
becoming nearly a stranger to himself. There are daily
affirmations, credos and proverbs, thoughts on meditation,
research on growth-stock mutuals, college funding and a
reading list void of the strategically brockeraged New York
Times bestsellers with exception to Tartt's quasi-dark **The
Goldfinch** I've been waiting on for 13 years. And not to neglect
honey-do-lists written to myself to improve the near and
distant future. I study them and others on a morning when high
winds batter the house, blow sequined waves of snowacross the
ghosted pallor of streetlights as my son, forever tardy, misses
the yellow Blue Bird once again. The commute to the middle
school is treacherous. I pull over twice for whiteouts. Gusts
rock the car like a twin Cessna tossed in high turbulence.In
moments like these, you understand life is mostly
unmanageable. At the school'sdrop-off Nathan joins the other
kids who trudge backwards against the wind." An Artic noose "
reports NPR on the way home, " descended from the desolate
prairies of Saskatoon ". *That's just beautiful* I hear myself say:

part cynicism, part dissbelief, partly out of fear knowing death
can arrive in the disguise of beauty from such a remote place. I
pull into our cul-de-sac where at the end of the drive the
windhas died down and the pewter clouds have parted revealing
the brilliance of a three-headed sundog in the frigid air. I make
note to make a note, add it to the collectionin the study, room
where the future is written out, waiting to be lived.

At the Greenwood Lounge

> *To communicate the agony of incommunication*
>
> — David Shields

Most nights the small flicker of a story or two:

what surfaces from pop culture or the locally

aggrieved, a small cruelty if told just right

will issue a string of empathy's laughter.

No personal tragedy or spurned love,

no emptiness or melancholy to blame

for stopping off after work, to find a home

before home, except to say, to plainly admit,

I like drinking here among the working stiffs.

But tonight I sit at the end of the bar

content in my darkened alcove, winter's frosted

glass narrowing my view across the street

at Gigi's Pilates where a straggle of pliant women trot

towards the heat and safety of their European sedans

and sport-cars. Behind me a couple of ragtags openly

discuss trafficking designer drugs, the paranoia and

possible legal ramifications. Then in a moment of

complete bathos, count off cribbage points and throw

back the last of their beers with drunken hilarity.

A few regulars come and go, take with them

their companionable gloom or contentedness.

A couple of stools away a certain patron

gazes into the bar-back mirror, stares into

himself, lost, meditative, perhaps lost in Zazen,

oblivious to the bottled liquors shining

like polished agates, the harmonica of Supertramp's

Long Way Home wheezing from the adjacent

pool room. Or, upon further inspection, is that me,

fifteen years ago, stoned with grief, staring

down the future, sure it didn't have a place

for me, unable to imagine a reason why

I should stand up and walk out, believing,

as I did, that I possessed two souls—

one which refused to speak to me, the other

which refused to listen to what I had to say.

Land of Bizarro

Inside the skirted fender, gravel ricocheted off the wheel
well, whizzed and pinged. Oh how it rang out, the spray
sounding like bullets missing the flesh of their intended
targets.I remember listening as I flinched from the trunk—
endorphin's rush of being smuggled into the Drive-In, a kid's
fantasy hatched in the dark. Tonight, on A&E, movie-making
that glorified the horror of living "The Sicilian Way"— that
gruesome scene from **Casino** where Pesci's *Santoro* is released
from tail-fins ,the Nevada stars burning overhead as some low-
level Mafioso hands him a shovel, orders him to dig a double
grave at gunpoint— one for him *and* his blindfolded brother.
It's moments like these where I flee by osmosis, disappear into
the land of bizarro— those Friday nights sneaking into the
Mason City Drive-In. How it felt so criminal, so *epiphanic*
escaping that cavernous shell I shared with a spare and a tire-
jack, to be helped from the trunk and handed a Coors— my
aunt's reward for the ten-year-old who endured the journey—
salty beverage that primed the pump for an evening's double-
feature of guts & gore, troubling addiction that would last a
lifetime But how unlike drinking to be *released* from that
oblivion, from above the signature badging, gangster
whitewalls of her '73 Coup de Ville, believing this must be
what the dead felt like, what it feels like to *be* dead— the key
unhinging the latch, the giant carapace swinging open like a
coffin's lid to reveal Orion tracking through the night sky,
reminding I knew nothingabout death or dying, nothing about
the monumental jolt of heartache that follows, nothing of loss
outside the movies,

any world beyond the scaffolding of the giant wooden screen—
not even the fact that the light that reached us arrived from a
place vanished long ago.

On the Other Side of the Monongahela River

Here's what's happened: my mother is leaving

                    the meager pay

of the *Des Moines Register & Tribune* for Allentown's

                    Morning Call,

for a doorman and a 12th story penthouse, for more

                    money than she

will ever make the rest of her life, for the Assistant

                    Editor's desk

where she can gaze at the waxy plumage of autumn

                    colors banded

like shiny filigree through the Blue Mountains,

a startling brilliance as

incomprehensible as to how she got here: college dropout,

divorcée, mother-

of-two who plies her amorous heart in the workplace, casts her

black magic

into the lives of married execs who promote her out of fear of

her sexual

withholding. This is her trade, my mother's ticket to the top.

She will shake

her hair out like Medusa's snakes, writhing vipers that entrance

and complicate

the souls of weak-willed men. Her unorthodox beauty cunning,

a vehicle for

sleeping her way into positions beyond her intelligence and

quailification.

It's 1980. My mother's '72 Peugot barely chugs through Ohio,

the smokey hills

of Pittsburgh with a fifth-wheel Uhaul in tow. On the

other side of the

Monongahela River a giant billboard holds the grizzly

stare of Mean

Joe Greene. He wants what's absent from his extended

ring-studded hand.

Below a rhyming epigram tells us so— *one for the thumb*

in '81. If only

words were truly prophetic. If only we had stayed in Iowa,

if only I could've

French-kissed Erin Petticourt in the furtive shadows through

the remainder of

8th grade, held her hips in the semi-dark beneath the grand-

stand, cavernous

alcove where we traded the unguent grease of her bubble

gum Lip Smacker.

By Christmas my brother and I have decided to make Mom's

life a living hell.

By spring we break her like a bridled mare. Worn thin, she

was out of options,

hopeful rejoinders, spirited repartees to our cruel comments,

constant

badgering, spiteful attempts to de-value her love. Come

summer she

sends us to stay with a man little practiced at being our father.

By the following

fall, she has fled to the human swamp of Manhattan, an

advertising gig her

lover arranged once management at the paper grew

disillusioned with

her charm, unearthed holes in her vitae she couldn't sufficiently

explain. Was she

ever the same? Were we? I'm thinking of the years my mother

has lived on

the lean, near poverty's serrated edge. Isn't it a good son's

charitable heart

the steps in, isn't it his moral imperative to do so? If so, what's

next?

The Pitfalls of Evolution

My therapist sighs, swallows the weight of the moment,

then clears his throat to ask, "Tony, what do you believe is the

fate of mortality?" Careful not to *own* an opinion, a

proof that might later be held against me, evidence submitted to

discredit my possible petition in the highest and holiest

of courts, a breach in contract that could be summoned by

heaven's writ, I fall mute to the white noise of my

continual dismay, mystery that dogs me from session to

session, crux of my dilemma T.J. has repeated for more

than a year, what he claims *is at the root of all my anxiety:*

a stupefying fear of the unknown, unimaginable void

of non-existence, a consternation that can be traced back to

the ancients, a people who catalogued the inexplicable

with charcoal drawings, our earliest forms of sophistry

that linked truth to the moon and stars, aid that

followed them to sleep through the night lest a saber-tooth or

woolly mammoth roused Paleolithic concern when the

coarse, animal silhouettes emerged in the cave's mouth and

children roughed images of terror and bloodshed

on the stone walls as they shied from the treacherous

moonlight.

Beneath the Bleacher's Din

Out walking the insect-churned dusk, I happen upon

the residual of the old field, stone and mortar stadium

where I spent Friday nights. Now the land is nothing but

fallow ground, weed and rock outcropping waiting on

commercial development. Summers like these they primed

the joint, slapped paint on the press box and concessions,

replaced wooden crossbeams and re-poured concrete footings.

When they played under the lights we watched from *under*

the bleachers, Erin Pettigrew and I, her tongued affection

permission to search for line & lace. As the hour falls to

darkness I walk the memory of the game's sight and sound,

what we witnessed from our shadowy enclave: boys spitting

rivulets of blood, the thunderous clap of pads, chests heaving

like bellows while coaches barked out praise or challenged their

sense of valor. That's when Erin would whisper beneath

the bleacher's din, her breath quickening as our team began to

mount a drive. She instructed me how to kiss and stroke, where

to place my hands, reminding me *this* was her favorite part,

careful not to unhinge her bra's clasp too early, release the

weight of her firm parabolas before our boys scored.

A maneuver tantamount to feeling, which made the moment

more climactic. At least that was the idea.

Googling Emily Dickinson

Words written on the hotel's embossed

stationary, an elegance framing solitary

solitary images I gathered from walks

on The Lake. Nothing arcane or fussy,

just simple moments that spoke to

or through me, a couple of stanzas that

felt fresh on arrival, words to start

my day abandoned to lamp-glow while

wife and boys slept and I slipped out

for coffee. Left on the desk: *From the wharf

I watch hawks glide on thermals, gulls ride

the crest of whitecap spray, pigeons search*

for crumbs as I walk the early vestiges of dawn,

listen to the perfect theorem of each wave's arrival,

each serpentine trough carrying the bitter hint

of death crash into the pylons below.

But upon return, scribbled beneath my tidy

work, a shorter attempt at verse decidedly more

uplifting, four lines written in my son's hand:
The lassitudes of contemplation/Beget a force/
They are spirits still vacation/That him refresh

Words written as if to say there are **two** poets

in this family, words written as if to improve on

my beach reflection, one-up my modest affair.

And though its language sounds vague and

old-timey, is composed of end-stopped lines

oddly compressed, like mine, it feels a want

of something more, as if a piece of itself

was left behind in the morning dark.

And when read to my waking wife (its appropriated

genius still undeclared), its voice sounded so

singular, so specifically itself, I shouted

" Anita, our boy's in touch with the muse.

His gift is off the chain !" But before I could

settle into literary flights of fancy, my life's

accumulation of mostly poetic shadow serving,

if nothing else, as a conduit to his greatness,

Nathan retrieved his I-Phone and smirked with

a "cat-ate-the-canary" glare, a secret knowledge

I'd been punk'd when he revealed his last Googled

entry, two lines omitted from the stationary because he

heard my return at the door: *The dreams consolidate*

in action—What mettle fair And though I knew I'd

been had, I recognized a simple joy of work in

those words, a hunger for *the experience,*

the only compensation an artist should ever seek.

What Emily herself thoughtfully composed,

possibly by candlelight one morning as she waited

for the sun to rise, for the golden disc to fill

her home with a more suffused glow. A light

she could take her weekly bath by, to lean

back and lower that famous bun to the water.

The Stuff of Legend

It goes without saying, I'm not the first alkie questioning his

decision to go on the lamb. Dry days of courage, pills designed

to regulate neuro-transmitters have failed miserably. Runner's

high, commitment to counsel's verbage are what have kept me

away, that and pilfered funds, early dispersals of my 401K,

notion that money spent, the accumulation of personal

affects, could be suitable collateral for the delusion I could

manage drink. I fault Mickey Rourke, his sleazy yet endearing

treatment of "Buk", how he made the drinking life seem gutty

and cavalier, an existence worth embracing as long as poetry

flowed and a woman of fidelity and bright constitution,

a woman with fine features and a spark of bravado, a woman

like Faye Dunaway was waiting for you. Pshaw! The over-

amplified rubbish of writing! The sick and manipulative

language of addicts! Historians of bad behavior, self-made

debauchery, how after a 3-day bender one could drift so far

from conscientious bearings that you, yes you, while your wife

was away, could sit a call girl in an oak rocker as your boys

dressed for school on the other side of the wall. And to think

a week earlier you stood before your woman's steely gaze,

lurch of a 115 lbs., and denounced, repeatedly, never ever

having relations outside the gold bands of trust. And did so

deadpan, with utter confidence, belief of one trapped in

the conundrum of pathology's maze. And now trembling

thought to come off this hiatus like swimming between jagged
reef of Scylla &Charibdis. Odds of surviving infinitesimally

small, dire %age according to the gurus of AA; chances better

at craps or roulette, a head-on at 60 mph, a major league fastball

flush in the face. But the empty savior is beguiling,

a treacherous lady singing in two part harmony, thunderous

ovation that rages in the veins. What to do, what to do? Jesus,

you wonder how the fuck you could allow yourself to ever

entertain. Know deeply the horrors, dark days of denial, how

perfected tricks of self delusion, embraced the mockery you

made of your life under its thrall. No matter. Desire will

enliven and revive. Dream can suggest and recall: arduous

laughter, clank of bottle and glass, how sumptuous meals were

waved away in favor of the blur of beverage. Come morning,

years removed from adolescent un and pleasure, the annotated

saga told by friend or family of all that went wrong. And yet

another headache, speculative bruise and banished

ego, flurry of sarcasm and mockery asides that ended with

removal from favorite restaurant by clownish pratfall.

Aubade/Serenade

> *Give me just another night, just another night with you,*
> *Give me just another kiss, just before the dawn breaks*
> *through*

> —Mick Jagger

An aubade, not in the French tradition of precious leave-taking

(the unbearable ache of young lovers parting at dawn,

the dread of the day's hours spent without love's searching

tongue or permissive grope), but to honor the calling of a high-

backed chair, morning's gift of empty hours when I can slum in

the quotidian, drift in the undulation, both jazz laiden

and orchestral, finch or whippoorwill, starling or warbler

crooning in the eaves and spring thicket laced with nascent

flowering. Those heartbeats pounding faster than gatlin gunfire,

calling shamelessly (for all we know) for the ministration of sex in looping units of measure, in ditrochee and dispondee,

in Latin roots that designate complexities of meter, the ratta-tat-

tat outburst of tetrasyllabics, frenzied bird jangle sweeping

through the tilt of morning's shadowy hour, song unfolding

beneath the cross-stitch of jet wash powdering the ether sky.

 At night, the glittering speck of fuselage is replaced with

the sliver of a carved-out moon, avarian pitch with my own

pining ache to deliver evening long— fabled serenade!

Beneath this same window I'll attempt to startle and woo,

amuse married half, parchment shadow of

shapely wife, calling out in mocking singsong of Grimm

fairytale: *Anita, Anita, let down your hair* as her

pulchritudinous silhouette is enhanced one article at a time undressing in the bedroom's lamplight, and I can't think of

without thinking of that lone evening in her campus

dorm-room, moment that parodied Jagger's MTV video: taut

leg bent in angled seduction, fingers smoothing ruffled anklet

then motioning an invitation to please and be pleased. Then a

dream after of tenured partnership, that decades later, unlike

the Beatles, we could still manage to *Come* (cum) *Together*.

Big Fun

Impossible to ignore these saucy pin-ups, even harder to take
them *for real*: era of whiskey flask and supper-clubs,
buffoonery of the 50's when big-bodied broads sang of a desire
to be filled with love before they returned to the table,

emblazoned tarts who've slunk across a half-century of branded
formatting from the golden years of Technicolor's flat
chicanery (saturated primaries transferred to Hollywood
lovelies on Westinghouse and Sylvania sets), to the resolute

brilliance of a new Sony LCD, how I'm bathed in waves of
stuttering light, though monochromatic, not the pixeled images
I see on-screen, ruse of platinum blondes who rollick
in their curvaceous expanse, generous haunches bunched in

satin, sparkle of jacquard sequin rising to meet the cinch of an
hourglass waist below the peaked country of tits— cupped
spillage poured into a pointy brassiere, that year's version of
Vogue more befitting of automotive design belonging to the

finned body of a Plymouth or Ford. But we can glom on to their
emotional insecurity, the swell of woodwinds and strings that
punctuate loneliness rising from the orchestral pit. O' for the
temerity of it all! These breathy sirens who sing songs that tug

at lust! Starlets of the silver screen who cast words and baited
eyes towards undeserving men— stock screw-ups, self-
contained moguls and the young, greasy Capones of the world
who blame their nomadic lechery on the misguidance of drink,

their hang-dogged look begging for a chance to be graced
by celestial bodies they only deserve to observe deep in the
night sky. And at the end of such songs, the arrival of a jigger
and cubed ice, a tumbler for the truth to be spilled at

the approach of the blanched faces of eternity, women long
dead before my midnight scrutiny: *Listen doll, sweetheart,
sugar, kiddo* a lexicon laced with strange entitlement, monikers
of sweetened innuendo uttered casually the approach

of filmed auras— Mansfield or Monroe— the impossibility of
shrinking from their medusa like come-hither, the voluptuous
bottom about to be dropped in their lap.

At the Mason City Drive-In

My aunt was the queen of adventure, had scaled
Half Dome, posed for *Playboy*, was the beer-chugging
champ of Iowa City where her photo hung
in The Airliner for years, so whenever "Crazy Lisa"
returned home to the lake, we had capital FUN:
water-skied, parasailed, rode bareback at her
boyfriend's estate, drank mini cans of Coors while
we practiced karate outside behind the stables—
mainly how to block a kick, deliver paralysis with a single
blow, whatever it took to ward off my worry, trick myself
into believing I could handle the bleakest of situations,
knew what to do if I stumbled into vortex or parallel dimension,
had to deal with the hissing terror of a *Sleestak*.
But Friday nights were reserved for the Drive-In
where we bypassed the parental guidelines
of the Motion Picture Association of America
by stowing me in the trunk of her '76 Coup de Ville.
Tonight on A&E, that gruesome scene from **Casino**—
Pesci peering from a trunk as the burn of Nevada stars
speaks to his fate. He's handed a shovel, told at gunpoint,
through his blubbering and asthmatic sobs, to start
digging his own grave. Memory uncoils like a dream,
as if embracing someone else's life: giant wooden screen,
metal cage of a speaker-box; the black and white promotional
posters tacked to the screen-door of the snack-bar
embellishing the experience of watching " Movies Under The
Stars"— the thrill and panic of being driven there in complete
darkness, how it promoted the circulation of morbid proclivities
how thinking about it now I flinch with each thud of gravel

spit under the wheel well— O' how they rang out, whizzed
like bullets missing their targets as I lay in that Cadillac coffin
waiting to be released, waiting on a familiar hand to haul
me out of oblivion, believing this must be what the dead
feel like, what it feels like to be dead before the trunk
flew open to reveal probing constellations, how even the light
that reached me might be "dead-on-arrival", starlight
arriving from a source that no longer existed. But it's only
the world waiting with its onslaught of time, the world
waiting to teach the infinite ways in which it can claim
through its silent auction of bidding.

Dear Departed

Tell us where you've gone, leaving us here
at your burial, questioning the eternal, defending
the notion of theodicy even though the simple
process of decay appears evil, your face beginning
to deliquesece to Jell-O, our faces beginning
to prune, to pucker and fall, age in obeisance
to gravity. Comforting to dream a sort of heaven,
dimension of unparalleled time and space,
vacuum where personalities are free to meet,
drift across centuries to speak, where even
adversaries like Bonaparte and Wellington
might chat light-heartedly about their legendary
reversals at Waterloo. Tell us where you've gone
as we walk the cemetery in our finest clothes,
touch gravestones warmed in the afternoon sun.
For a while a dignified silence on the hill
where staggered slabs are etched with names
as we don't know until sound breaks below—
muffled chink of a struck golf ball followed
with expletives, an exasperated plea, another
soul trying to hack its way out of a deep lie.

Déjá Vu 1978

there we are, standing on the roof
of Stilwell Jr. High, small stones sinking under

our heels in the warm pitch like back-road macadam,
maroon daubs of sunset oozing through the picket

trees from where, we could only guess,
came the nighthawks— the reason we scaled

the school walls, suffered the brick and mortar joints
that bled our hands and knees.

To disturb and be disturbed, to be in the presence
Of their screeching dives, how each time we thought

they'd truly wing us. And so it is tonight
with the martins that wheel and dive,

tack and turn towards the grass-top hungry
for moths that hatch and flutter into the evening air.

A .and I hold reserves of wine, stemware filled,
near the color of memory, the backdrop of night

some thirty summers ago like F-14's in Vietnam newsreel.
A different world then, for some, when so much

more must have seemed at sake. The swallows hover,
plummet with grace, return emotion to a pristine state,
however briefly.

Beatlemania Lives

The Summer of Love, a season that lives
        for me in moniker alone, in dated sepia,
rock n' roll documentaries where footage
        from that nether world is aired on A&E.
Dire fact: this summer Sgt. Peppers and I
        turn 52. What's more half the Beatles
have been dead for years, and in August,
        by the numbers, I'll have mounted
the ascent into middle age. Ah, the feeling
        for what will not return, a place we
did or did not exist. And here's the original
        album cover dusted and drawn from
a basement crate, grooved vinyl worn smooth
        when I subscribed to psylosybin, musty
mushroom which warped time and space, infused
        sound with color. Fresh from my teenage
archives here are the mustachioed Beatles
        resplendent in their day-glow getups,
chartreuse, saffron, baby-blue and tangerine
        uniforms replete with military insignias,
metal buttons and fringed epaulettes.
        They appear serious next to their waxed
brethren, the happy-go-lucky mod-squad
molded by Madame Tussauds. They poseas impresarios,
maestros of a new sound,

a militia band clutching wind instruments,
music that called for the arrangement
          of embrouchure. Truth be told, I haven't
listened to the album in years, though yesterday,
          while gassing at a local convenience,
I saw their lyrics take unprecedented form:
          Bounding through the station's door
The words *Guaranteed to Raise a Smile* printed
          across a woman's ample chest. A reference
now forever changed, a motto loaded
          with sexual potency. As a younger man
I might have winked, teased with mention
          of something vulgar, asked for further
evidence. But today I'll just slide the ethanol
          with hers', my smirk confirming her approaching
promise to deliver.

Feign & Cut

Indian summer a shroud of humidity that hangs in the form of
crystalline vapor over the striped field. Flaming sun falling
backside, burning from a ridge Of distant pine. Its ruby
trajectory caught in a canvas of heaped-up clouds, firey

arms sweeping the diorama of altocumulous folding and
unfolding in the cinematic light. I survey Nathan's practice
under such brilliance, my helmet-headed son shirking my
exhortations, my words of encouragement met dead-on-arrival

by his hard eyes from the fringe of the huddle. Coach's whistle
again: **the snap's on two boys on two!**Halfback in motion,
trotting through a cadence of hard counts knowing ultimately
(barring disaster of timing, the center's untimely flinch or

transfer of ball) the pigskin is meant for him, a play designed to
use his gifted speed. I raise my nose from review, from my
sister-in-law's disturbing texts: *ur brother showing up to Mac's
practices drunk again! Hounding me 4 $, home cooked meals…*

all this after I left 18 months ago! Finally the execution coach
has been looking for as the ball exchanges hands three times
before crossing the line of scrimmage. Then her texted follow
up: *fuk'd in the head… needs ur help! problems with gait*

and sleeping limbs. Still he continues 2 drink! From the narrow
street cars pop and chirp, security sounded from the sidewalk,
from the lime-green grass recently seeded behind the end zone
where a straggle of parents wait in silence. It's an end-around,

the only play   I ever scored on in middle school. I remember
the clandestine nature of the huddle, The nervous apprehension
when Danny Webber called "my play". My first thought not to
score, but not to **fail**, fumble the ball under coach's hawking

eye. But this boy's work seems effortless, a pallid face of ease
and determination as he bounds downfield, switches the tuck of
the ball from inside to outside arm as he scoots across the has
marks, gallops with a strange fluidity. Steel screech,

authoritative blasts calling for an end to the play, an end to
practice as a string of boys pat-down congratulations
On his oversized pads. A squadron of geese arrow overhead.
The musky scent of fall rises from the wooded lots. The last

dregs of daylight granular on the horizon, kaleidoscopic, an
almost manufactured swirl— topaz, aubergine, apricot and
claret, brassy golds drowning in the sea-green above the boy
who scored as he comes jogging up: Sinatra-eyed poseur, smug

kid who has torn the helmet off his sweat-drenched locks,
eyeing me quizzically, approaching my joy-stretched face,
maybes surprised that I'm surprised, that it's him, my son, who
can sprint through the world like this, feign and cut, slither

through a hole before he barrels into daylight.

Sonnets & Bref Doubles

Ancestry.com Informs of Relation to Huck Finn

By now you know you can't have it all,
but along the way nobody told
me what that meant or looked like. To be
honest, I was never explained much of anything.
And by the time logic, good senses took hold,
it was too late. So far behind the eight-ball,
I decided *scruples* didn't apply. Bold
meant LIVING, no matter if you're "pissing"
it away. "Obeyance" meant you had no gall,
and that was no fun coming from a household
that shirked parental roles like the plague. On an atoll,
marooned, we never looked for help. Latch-key
kids are clever, vagrant, little Tom Sawyers with balls
bigger than hearts. Life a cinch no matter how crappy.

Small Talk (The American Way)

In a conversational pinch, one could always turn
        to talk of family, local weather or sport,
holiday on the calendar's horizon. But best to spurn
        the tragedy of national news, shock of Fort

Hood, even if tempered with equal measures of grief
        and pathos. In the presence of a stranger,
if stumped, if anxiety had wrested away the belief
        in a common ground, or one was mired in anger,

these subjects considered a safe play. But talk is cheap
        in a country that mirrors a neurosis it engenders. Flat
comments surely hide troubled thinking. Political creed
        best kept off the street. If you feel taken back,

heap shame online, make innocence your bitch or goat.
        Everybody knows value of a soul is measured by it vote.

Writing on the Surface of a Wave

—for Jamie Leigh

Effaces itself, unlike words on a page where god
Or the goddess of monogamy could rap
To question selfish pangs of the heart.
What is unrequited love? Outside
Plath or Berryman, nary a clue. Then the map
Of your pinned location arrived and thawed
Feeling forgotten since high school. The gap
In our friendship over 30 years! *Abide
By social graces*, I tell myself. But it's only a façade
To this thrust of emotion, witting trap
That circumvents logic like finding love abroad.
Obviously, you can only push this so far—
But there she is: whip-smart, sassy; a lightening rod
For lust or love. And me? The fool playing his part.

From Reubens to Rembrandt

With the faintest musing I look upon
The morning hour suffuse with color;
From the burgeoning of lavender and cream
(Softball-sized hydrangea), to slender
Necks of zinnia which wave and flutter
In the marine breeze (their brilliant pawn
Of carmine, sapphire and hue of butter-
Cup seduce the eye in their vibrant splendor).
And before I know it, I've lapsed into daydream
Where I imagine myself the executor
Of some Flemish estate that attracts the wonder
Of its beauty for modest fees— a tender
Paid for the masters of oil in the Halcyon
Days when art mirrored life. Everything in between.

Any Lunker
                    -for Matthew Bruce Panek

Here goes nothing said with a shrugged shoulder,
Then he whipped a jigger from above his waist.
It wasn't the best of Sundays. Cold,
Windy, rainy. Clouds floated by like petroglyphs,
Marauders from the underworld. But haste
Wasn't in the forecast. And now that we're older,
There's life to catch-up on, memory erased
By years, pitted like the bauxite cliffs
Rising from the water. In a perfect mold
(10 o'clock to 2 o'clock), your rod will trace
Infinity as I lean starboard to chase
Down a loose beer. But you prefer gifts
Unbidden, thrash of Cat or Sauger.
Any lunker that breaks the drag truth be told.

Brigand

Sunday morning just before 9, the low-
throated growl of a vintage, powder-blue
Charger inching down the ravine. Minutes later
a '59 Eldorado with fins and gangsta
white walls follows. All it takes are those two
Hunnies to muscle under a fanned ginko
holding a brood of European cuckoo
(loosely referred to as an asylum— bourgeois
descendants that clamber in iambic chatter)
to spring me like "Chief" at the end of *One Flew
Over The Cuckoo's Nest*. Any name you choose
to define makes no difference to me. What I saw
in the hoosegow last night made a john doe
out of me forever. Only vodka cranberries hereafter.

Pissed

Unequivocally, it's her last stand.
She has no room left for *phases*. Won't tolerate
liars, alcoholics, cheats— anyone who can't muster
a penchant to save themselves definitely
not a person worthy of being her *mate.*
And how could I argue or force my hand?
To be honest with myself is to backdate,
to admit actions selfish and lackluster
to say the least. The intrinsic nature of its weight?
To admit it's me whose compounded our fate
by refusing to accept my recusancy.
Since I got the slip, I'm all bog and quicksand,
beer and whiskey. A bonafide knuckle duster!

After an Exposé on Southern Culture, 14 Years Later,
God Reveals His Reasons for Katrina

The fate of a city— gratuities given
to these denizens for two centuries thrown
away over greed and neglect. Riven
souls bestowed with my greatest loan:
wrought-iron porticos and jazz, creole
and French cuisine; musical dipthongs courtesy
La Louisiane before the steely ego
of timber barons practiced mercy
as a surcharge for using the waterway.
Now a city of graffiti art, shelled
buildings and maudlin decay. What's deserved
goes without saying. I felt compelled
to keep the Superdome for a tent city. Preserved
the French Quarter on an apostle's nudge.
Whoever said God couldn't hold a grudge?

Welcome To Your Life

A single cottonwood seed aloft in
The crystalline sunshine, in the glaze of a perfect
Day. In a moment like this, if you sit
With supreme attention, you'll find the world basks
In triumphant light even when it's bedecked
With misery and shadow. You'll only begin
And end a handful in a lifetime— select
Offerings that find you just so, when skin
Bristles and joy shudders along the spine. Time befit
For angelic sighs, the muazzin's call to connect.
State of pure being. Buoyancy that takes effect
Without your knowing. If somebody asks
For real?, tell them something to make their head spin.
Tell them being is nothingness. All *else* counterfeit.

Suicide Psalm

The hour frozen in its drowsy beauty—
        four geese, a quantifiable gaggle, row
across the morning sky— its blue bounty
        by the contrast of a distant,

soot colored squall gathering, almost
        incredulously, on the horizon. But for
now the world is tranquil, a pleasant host,
        the pitch of the moment at its dreamy core

enough to alleviate the fear in the ever
        tenuous gyre of mortality. After all,
its only our own ghosts that await, clever,
        well-schooled authorities on the pall

of living forever. Hungry for company they stray
        from the shadows, anxious to lure us away.

Our House

He blamed his rage on his heritage—
Cretian blood equaled Cretian temperament:
anger that required fistfuls of sedatives,
slugs of whiskey to insure the *betterment*

of its effects, though he'd just sleep it off.
Our house more than theater, more than
a show— a place of one continual standoff
after another, where what's done is **done**.

Dad made sure mythic barbarism came
To life. So after a cupped palm came the strap,
or whatever could turn a young hide aflame,
make him think twice before giving crap.

History used as a provocation, excuse
to deliver blows. But don't *dare* call it abuse

Starring Role

thy eternal summer shall not fade
—Shakespeare

Attention received on a floodlit stage
not enough (foil characters of *Hamlet*
and *Macbeth*, derelict villain portrayed
in a campy Vaudeville skit), offstage a magnet

for troubled roles; scenarios never read
in poems or plays, my strange appetite
for trafficking in the commerce of greed
most beguiling. Cursed with a hedonist's delight.

Those speed-fueled nights. Ill-fated, unlucky
kid we rolled for dope, a running engine.
From fingerprint files to cuffs to juvy—
a fool's walk. High drama with true suspension.

Once, atop the municipal high dive, I froze
in a cop's searchlight. Drained my beer. Then dove.

Natural World

Warmest fall on record. Weather never displayed
        in these parts. Indian Summer kept
under a golden blanket till Pilgrim's Day.
Now this: grass freeze-dried, burlapped

in a slag heap of orange and umber,
        fresh bruise of a churlish sky. Wind spawned
a mess of things. Up and down the street clumps
        of refuse: shingles, siding, patio chairs wrested

like weak paperweights. A plastic bag
        snaps in homage to a lost season.
By the front step a rumpled Yankees cap
        cartwheels a Goldfinch nest. High treason.

Outside hands, feet go numb. Better to stare
through hoarfrost. Let wind inhabit poems, prayer.

I digress…

How many years will I clamor to get
this right? For as long as I could stand
music has been my godsend, how I could see
and feel my way into the soul. Please believe
me (or PLEASE PLEASE ME— I digress to that band
nobody can stop talking about, who beset
the world in a siege, coup d'etat of such grand
force the world could never hope to achieve
those dizzying heights again) when I say the key
to happiness is like writing in the sand—
though you mark grit, perpetuity will demand
you give it away. To think otherwise to deceive
the self like a socialist or politician, or that "that" brunette
will return to sing "Oh Darling, please believe me…"

My Participation in the *Internal Family Systems Therapy*
Sessions Every Other Wednesday @11am

3900 Ingersoll— suite of offices where I park
        every other Wednesday under the same tree,
ride the carpeted Otis up to the third (where on a lark
        I started coming in hopes it would unlock the mystery

of my drinking sprees), and thumb through *Psychology*
        Today waiting for my name to be called, then
walk the short hallway to the room where the ontology
        of my behavorial and spiritual maladies is penned,

probed and prodded by T.J.'s practiced ease.
        And this for six years and counting: the delicate
disternment of my psyche. Like *Operation*, each piece
        teased out, taking the whole apart bit by bit

so we can examine the wellspring of multiple selves.
Each voice part of a family, speakers silenced by twelve.

Betrothal

Neither one of us reached for the snooze-bar,
        but let the sound of rock n' roll play
as we drifted between dream and that far
        shore, subcutaneous level, middle space

where you lay connected to two worlds at once.
        And when we emerged from that sweet state,
the pure shock of what we hadn't done,
        neglected to "do" when we overslept

our honeymoon's scheduled flight— gossamer train
        still tied, garter clamped to thigh,
boutonnier petals on your negligee.
        Knowing we forgot to fuck you cried.

Waltzing through a ballroom has it affects.
After drink and dance what should one expect?

During A Rehab Meeting Joseph Conrad Comes To Mind

We know what we've got: the Black Plague bottled
genetically. The trick is not to let the genie
out: three wishes one-in-the-same to get throttled,
faded to the core. In the endgame, even Houdini

could only pick so many locks. So once a week
this collection of misfits gather. Nothing
of the anonymous sort; we honor **and** critique,
call out by nickname or surname putting

our disease in perspective when we lose sight.
There's *Esquire* and *Bennis, Ray-Ray* and *Stein,*
a teacher, a cop and yours truly. A gifted playwright
couldn't have scripted it better. Genesis of bloodline

brings us together. *Heart*(s) *of Darkness* in search
of relief. Grace not found in drug or drink; awkward lurch.

Of Thousands: An Eternal Lament

The Bibbs' eastern windows are slate-grey,
        except the gable's triad which has caught
the sunrise in panorama, display
        of molten light— three dizzying spots

where color between volcanic red
        and canary yellow a bomb gone off—
fiery fusillade, end-time spread
across glass where I imagine heavy loss

 and hell's ruin; then heroic dream—
        climbing through toppled layers of steel,
pulverized concrete and smoking I-beams—
        to rise into a shattered cathedral

once a lobby's façade. None ever did.
Besides the rapture, eyes forever hid.

Part 3: Departure

In Training

That damned dog can't control himself: whimpers

and cries, skulks and moans until I rise under

the copper flush of dawn and shuffle down

the hall sleepily, muttering expletives in reference

to all hounds. My creaky footfalls send him

berserk in his cage where he yelps, barks, and paws

at the metal gate in a fit of delirium. Kenneling,

what dog enthusiasts call it, a euphemism to shadow

the heart from the nature of its small design,

from which I take him onto the lawn so he can do

his business, this butter-bean of a pooch, huffing

and snorting, barreling his snout into frosted

tufts of grass where each blade runs deep

with the thick scent of ambrosia.

I untangle his chain from the tree, wrestle

with my impatience remembering what you said

about the necessary trials of training, how I've

put you through the shredder from time to time

with my tomfoolery, my unwarranted theatrics,

evenings dispensed through the titillation of booze.

This morning you sleep comfortably in a bed

we've shared for twenty-two years, but I want you awake,

I want you out here praising *me* for not

giving up on this terrier in the early morning

fog where the red fruit of the chokecherry

floats with invisible suspension

and the ripple of the aspen is a sound

that can't be seen overhead. I want to be told

by the one who knows me best,

that apart from my shortcomings,

whatever misery I borrow from,

return to the world, that though the dog

continues to sniff and snoop, dig and furrow

ignoring my exasperated pleas for him to go,

that though the fog has turned to a cold rain

and my hands are cleansed red and raw,

I stay out here urging him on, thinking happy thoughts,

that this is good for me, so doggone good.

Replacements

Once again, the Douglas Fir is hauled out of the basement, a
steerage muscled, drug through narrow confines, tight corridor
framed by the furnace's stacked metal sheeting and the squat,

frozen cavity of the deep-freeze, chilled storage that hasn't been
filled with butchered goodies since Skogland's Meat Locker
moved in '09 two counties west of here on Highway

44. Verdant synthetics are then pulled apart, sectioned to
maneuver the hard, left angles of our stairwell. Minced version
of " troll the ancient Yule tide carol " sung with mocked

aversion as each dust covered branch of the fake is lifted
through the doorway where my wife waits in ritual with a
plastic sprig of mistletoe. Sensing my sardonic mood, she leans

in two-faced; one with a pert smooch, the other with breathy
words spoken like a headmistress behind closed doors: ***don't
you dare fuck this up for the children!*** After assemblage

and dressing, we step back to admire ornamental accrual. Of the
mass we single out the little drummer boy cast in knockoff
crystal, the angel's sagging weight spray-painted gold and the

earth's most commercial symbol of peace, oldest ornament
received as a kid— "genuine" porcelain dove engraved with
holiday's namesake: *Christmas 1978*. Across the road that day

(behind the white picket fence we used as a javelin in summer
to skewer dissected bird and frog heads' like they were waiting
for shrikes), the lumberyard ceased groaning, so Elvis

and Sinatra crooned from the portable turntable as the adults
got scotched-up. That year Santa appeared in the back entry

and winked behind his wool wig and beard. Though grandpa
was absently forgotten, old St. Nick stood steadfast in strange,
yet comely assurance. *Merry Christmas, little boy!* he belted

out, though the long syllables were ever elongated, and the hard
consonants tuned to mush— one long river off the slur of his
tongue.

The Mirror

After a close shave and rinse, foundation is applied.
Then eye-liner, eye-brightener,

clotted globules of mascara to heighten (or hide) my
features. Dressing, my feet

become entangled as I almost trip stepping into fishnets,
recover in time to hoist their

elasticity over seamless panties (picked-out by my wife
at Target), then round my

brassiere with mid-cup falsies and drop a sequined
Flapper over my head. Capezio flats

are chosen (reluctantly) instead of heels (as we know,
there are physical restrictions

when it comes to balance and grace of an *oafish brute*),
though to compensate

(a nauseating abomination that rolls across my sons'
teenage faces) I practice posture

and gesture, stroll and strut, how to strike a persuasive
pose as I think of that all that is

delicious in the feminine's possessive— power of allure,
command of sway, how the

titivate thrall can manifest itself in emotional commerce
and dependence. And I haven't

even voiced character yet! I return to the mirror for the
finishing touches: banded plume

of feather, blonde pageboy wig, *birthday babe* lip-liner
smacked into perfection as I

douse myself in waves of Pantene firm and say in dead
vernacular, in my best Jazz Age

lingo, as I stare deeper into the mirror and lift my chin
with incomparable comportment:

atta girl, **now** *your're an air tight smarty!*

When We Say *Nyet*

Greetings Comrades, please don't mistake this reference
as insult, salutation made famous by decades of hardliners. I
feel it still embodies the spirit our Motherland, solidarity

of a people who know meaning of sacrifice, who don't allow
our conditions to leverage our souls, who know true enemies
of the State control the Politburo, make the Parliament sing

and dance, guide their invisible strings like crazy petrushka.
Believe me when I say I've seen carnage first hand,
watched blood trickle into gutters like Hollywood movie.

No matter if you keep heart open for the State, if you put
what's best for it ahead what's best for you, if indignation
is channeled into complacency, because all thought or action

seen in opposition could make you available to Putin's
black magic, unfavorable trick of making people disappear
in front of open eyes. Dear Citizens, allow me to address you,

please know if this note should survive me or fall into
bad hands it wasn't written for vain. Allow me to speak
for what I know, these things available like, how do you say,

Behold Litvienenko's tea siphoned from secret samovar,
crushed leaves brewed with polonium-210;Natalia
Estemirova's bullet filled brain, body found in woods by her

house days after she publish about Putin's goons. How can one
look away from toppled mess, lives of Markelov and Barburova
dumped like like so much trash along street, or walking home

on frozen afternoon from Izmailovsky market I never forget.
Carrying bag of wooden Babushkas for my beautiful nieces—
modern girls who enjoy my ideas of joke, think it silly when I

give old-time trinkets— thought of their joy and laughter
vanish when I turn corner, walk into Kremlin's icy shadow to
find people standing over white face of Boris Nemstov. Tell

me, how to live with such things, how to live in a country of
such enormous power and resource, where if you act in outrage
then you must fear for your life. This is big problem, no?

Is there nothing we can do? Glasnost and Gorbache now like
empty dream, so many miles lost in rearview.
To think to live in place where such acts still committed

for names of those who perished during Great Patriotic.
My Comrades, is there no end in sight? And to think
Our lost brother Baryshnikov busies himself these days

speaking about *threat* of *Amerians* living in such ways.
My friends, I laugh when I hear these things.
Has he forgotten where he's from? And to think

they bicker and fight over this a slap to our face.
"Much Ado About Nothing" their British cousins
favorite saying. To lose one's mind over immigrants,

a wall to keep people *out,* to defend the *rights* of a fetus
to become mad at President Trump's Tweets,
to argue a right to take *marijuana* when all you

need to forget is a bottle or two of good Beluga?
We'd love to have your troubles and more! It would
be considered a balm for the soul! So next time,

Dear Citizens, you read or hear about Americans
whining, complain about this or that, remember they know
nothing of our troubles, nothing of our kind of

persecution, nothing of mind games we must play
day to day in order to survive, nothing about
the truth behind why we say *nyet.* Not to be rude,

but to hide what we are told not to feel.

L'escarpolette

Swinging, in the painting, her eyes meet the boutonniéred suitor
reclined among

        the rich overgrowth. He reaches out, face
imbued with the same raspberry shade as the flower stuck to his
lapel. His face flushed in awe, in the ecstasy of dream,

       of how he would chuff and shudder, of how she would
gasp and groan. But the *true* story isn't what was painted,
because her *true* love waited off-canvas, sweated

       nervously in the mansion's dusty vestibule. A
timid boy from school come to

      court with the standard of chocolates and fresh-picked
flowers. Years later will he

      come to know her Achilles heel: his sweetum's
love of endearing pet names, taste for sugared dates, soufflés
and wine. But Jean-Honoré had a taste for

     the bombastic, for what was irreverent, for what was
culturally taboo. So he paints

      the story of a beautiful temptress holding out by
refusing royal lineage,

by flirtatiously refusing a king's call from
birthright and money, gold trinkets

and an amethyst choker unknowingly stuffed in his
son's pocket where he called

from the forest floor. And now to stare at the
pixeled high resolution: Wikipedia's porthole of light striking
her bergére hat, columned shaft

probing her ruffled frock, softening the deeper folds to
saffron, labial pink as she is

swung higher and higher into the subtle
brilliance of that famous Fragonard,

smoky light once applied by an ox-haired brush and
daring imagination, a desire to master perfection exactly 200
years prior to the year of my birth.

But even more startling, the conspiratorial
undertone of the prized painting;

a stone angel's look of shock or disbelief, a
foregrounded monument of a winged

cherub who has drawn a finger to its pursed lips as if to
shush the impulse of what should be thought or said, if only
through me, in a moment of pure ekphrasis.

The perfect moment? You'd agonize a lifetime
waiting on it, an eternity without

ever receiving its kiss. So why not take morning's
robin-egg sky

and be on your way? Truth is the creation of a
story behind the painting made a better painting. Iconoclasm
used as an antagonist deepening the attention of the world's

eye. So why not

have the flummoxed prince gesturing from his
lay. Why not

have the stalwart girl play with his desire by kicking her
shoe off with a laugh. As the painter's story went: nothing he
could do or say influenced her.

Nothing would lure or entice.

No entreaty, no amount of overture or
outrageous promise, nothing whatsoever could persuade

la jeunefille to lift her ass

from the swing that ignominious day!

Heirloom

It's more or less her nipples set in aureoles
        the size of Kennedy dollar coins
visible beneath her lampshade blouse that
        caused all the fuss. Collectors of the day
scorned her reveal, labeled it *blasphemous,*
        predatory, an *indulgence* on point
with today's hardcore erotica this Royal Dux
        maiden, modest figurine, ceramic
of the 18th century simply a model of European
        peasantry holding bucket and jug
part of my wife's little treasure trove, small posse
        of figurines assembled on her dressing table
like that black & white of Grace Kelly's boudoir
        in Monaco I saw decades ago in the pages
of Life magazine— it's exquisite craftsmanship,
        shadow play of color and Anglican provenance
rarer than the Armada's gold bullion sunk off
        the coast of Spain. For generations she'd
been simply referred to as *The Girl*— article of reparation
        confiscated and returned twice from Germany;
once by Chancellor Theobald Von Bethmann-Hollweg's
        Pickelhelms, and then from the stone-cold Nazi SS.
From there she crossed The Atlantic after the war in the putrid
        hull of the MS St. Louis rife with thievery and lust.
After that she survived 2 house fires, a flood and an F5
        that flattened Marysville like the advancing wall
of an atomic wave. And still that wasn't the end of it,
        after being plucked before auction of my great aunt's
estate, on a neighbor's tip, we found her in the bay

window of Solar's Pawn & Loan, recovered after explaining to
        the owner it was hawked surreptitiously to feed my
19 year-old nephew's 3 year opioid addiction. But only days
        after brokering the exchange, I return home one evening
to find my wife sobbing as she stared dumbly at the floor,
        at *The Girl* fractured into a dozen pieces— mistake
of nerves, outlier of spring thunder causing the hand's reflexive
        twitch to undo centuries of survival. And just when
I thought her despair inconsolable, what could take months
        for my wife to absorb the heartache, she brushed away
her tears with the corner of her blouse, knelt to the floor,
        and began to gather the macabre of its broken
pieces before she did her best to glue The Girl back
        together again. If not a victim of survival before,
surely now a suitable stand-in, a symbol of desire
        disdain *and* wreckage; the attrition of time,
like repurposing, that creates its own appeal. In her own
        words, *neverdid ruin look so beautiful.*

Dirty Sweet

Nostalgia begins to do its rueful work when the captive thrallof
T.Rex comes on the radio: *you're dirty sweet and you're my*

> *girl,* cultural idiom of the possessive never thought of
> possessively, but in the manner of lust, of belonging

together. After class T. Ramirez and I would "steal time" in our
homestead's ramshackle garage where Dad preserved his

> broke-down *beauties*— a two-tone Fiat named Fiasco
> and a cobwebbed Karmann Ghia that threw a rod my

freshman year. Beneath a moss-fuzzed stone, the key that
unlocked the two-stahl door. Without a dash hardwired for

> sound, I spun the knob on an cathedral Philco
> stashed between a row of rusted paint cans. We'd sit

in the duct-taped seats, roll down the windows, and listen to
the British lilt of its strange idiom: *you got a hubcap diamond*

> *star halo, you're built like a car oh yeah.* In there time
> kept from others, time kept from across the brick street

when the First Presbyterian tolled on the hour. Between two
peals, all we could peel: covet of teenage lust and love;

to practice, in the near dark, what our friends lyingly
bragged about. We thought we lived beyond suspicion,

but to truly cover our tracks we'd have to undust the dusted.
Afterwards, we wore the studious faces of commerce,

of homework in the kitchen. Hovering over books, we
tried to sell the plutonic story studious junkies.

We feigned difficulty comprehending semantics, just how to
apply Ms. Bennett's chalkboard scribble, her lecture notes on

Shakespeare's use of the present perfect, what he meant
to have loved.

The Monarch's Diplomats

> — *el degüello* is a Spanish expression that
> translates to the English equivalent of *no quarter*

Gesturing from beneath his red parasol, shading himself

    from the sun and the Jungle's earlymorning heat,

    our tour guide, Nacho, informs us, " Their galleons

were anchored just beyond here". We stand and listen,

    drain bottles of Dasani and juice snagged in

    the parking lot gift shop just outside the crumbling

walls of the 2,300 year-old city.Beneath Nacho's outstretched

    hand, tireless waves that ridethe surf until they dissolve

    into sequined foam on the crowded beach.

"As they approached the shore ," he tells us, "their brass

telescopes spied the chiseled portholes of El Castillo

where they saw the dark eyes of my people

squinting back By *they,* he means the Spaniards, by *my* he

means the Mayans, indigenous people from which

he's descendant— a lineage traced back through

centuries a bloodline that built these limestone structures.

Most of our party lags behind, their interest waning in

the rising heat, lost with each new wrinkle, each new

sub-plot to Nacho's rendition of history, of how the

Conquistadores made shore. I pinch myself

to concentrate as he explains how they launched

themselves from the flotilla sheathed in metal carapaces, armor

replete with glinting rapiers and matchlocks.

Walking the ruins of Talum, you can almost hear

the plaintive shrieks of ghosts, vanquished souls calling out

from the limestone walls, cries of those who'd refused

to repent or submit, who couldn't make sense of

The Spaniards' thick broque or how their people had failed to

appease their Gods. But today, despite the stultifying

heat, joy seen wading into the peninsula's ocean

view: children frolicking in waves, their laughter drawn out

to sea on the welcoming breeze. The curvature

of earth bends towards the horizon on

the Caribbean's ship-less water. And then the dark thought

circles back, the terror of this place before it

had the look and feel of history, before tourists

swamped the land and imperialism's ugly truth announced itself

as it approached the Yucutan— ruthless war chant of

el degüello, el degüello as the monarch's diplomats

sashayed through the breakers.

Pops, Dis Playa Need Ta Roll

They leave home singing, return home singing,
iPhones providing a soundtrack to their days
as they overdub the lyrics with an aggressive,
more frenzied version of their own.
But *singing* is not right, not in the technical
sense of the word, an unqualified misnomer
that would have traditionalists seething
in their graves— sonorous crooners who
devoted their lives to perfecting the range
of their sound; signature vocalists like Holiday,
Pavarotti or even good olé Blue Eyes;
their throats emotive as any instrument.
How modulation of timbre transports
feeling into worlds unknown, even a single
note rolled in glissandro can transfix.
But my boys could care less about that—
Music as a vehicle, spiritual medium with
transformative power. My desire to be
moved lame as the word *gobbledygook.*
Their base requirement visceral; rap the body
can feel, words that rise defiant, defendant;
brash sentiment carried mostly on the wing
of bass and rhyme. After dinner my son
pimps in his self-affected gangsta: *Pops,
dis playa need to roll… I got beats to make
this nigga feel like drippin.* Then he thumps
his chest with an inverted peace-sign.
Smiles thinly. Scrolls through graphic
soundbites on iTunes rapping over the top

of his favorites: Tupac, 2 Chainz, Biggie
and Wiz; ownership meant to impress.
He tells me *Rock is dead*. I think to counter,
wish to tell him he's got it wrong, there's
much more to music than *this*. But thinking
is where it starts and ends.

Eclipse with Reference to Albert Pujols

Under the immense curve of the Arch's ghost-shadow, we're
able to peer into the cloudless sky without hand or brim and

admire its gleaming breadth. I'm dumbstruck, flush with
vertigo and awe, a mindless mess held together as Saarinen's

seamless joints support the massive tonnage of these steel
plates, as the perfect math used to cross-sect 630 feet and

the physics of its penumbra shading me in the blazing afternoon
are the same. But my boys are nonplussed, even after I point to

the tiny windows lost in sun-strike, the apex observation where
perhaps they're being watched: my two sons like ants, two

indiscriminate figures that kick off flip-flops and sprint the
Gateway's esplanade from base to base, four times over.

And I remember the Zapruder-like film of its construction on
YouTube— animated frames of early 60's black and white, the

creepers inching up the centenary legs, cranes positioned from
their support dropping in one steel triangle at a time, the gritty

jump-cut and the mechanical whirl of the projector, stunted
turn-of-the-century brick and mortar, the Old Courthouse,

the replica Roman basilicas and worn cathedrals in the
backdrop making the architecture even more Space Age.

Now the soldered bases have been dulled by grease, names and
dates, clichéd mottos of love and the vulgarity of love's

possession etched into the hulking metal meant to
commemorate a new frontier before steamers and barges,

Napoleon's land where only scrub and bramble skirted swollen
banks, where my children come to me panting, sweat-peppered,

thirsty, gasping, "Dad, is this it? Is this all there is?" followed
by reasonable queries: "When are we leaving?" "How far to the

stadium?" "When we get there, can we have something to eat?"
"Can we meet The Machine?"

Hailstones

No precursor of rain or wind, distant

thunder or ceremonial lightening strike,

no siren's blare or TV's pageantry of warning's,

not even a sense of atmospheric change,

acrid smell of ozone leaking in,

just the sudden burst of hailstones

that caught us dumbfounded in the yard.

Pea-sized, at first, they barely stung.

But they quickly swelled, and flinching,

we ran for safety under the soffit's overhang.

The storm, if you could call it that, ended

as abruptly as it began, and soon my boys

were picking iced-marbles from the lawn.

They dropped them in their mouths

like frozen berries, milky pearls of hard candy.

Their eyes widened. Across their faces

swept goofy grins. Treats, they think,

sent from another world.

If Only

Of the 60's, all I recall are its cartoon reruns in the 70's,

namely *The Jetsons*. I watched that kooky, space-age

surrogate family in my underwear, my brother and I eating

Funyons for breakfast sprawled on the carpet of our ground-

level apartment while Mom worked the opening shift at

Things, Things & Things. That fantasy world revealed

nothing of the world we lived in. Tidy, presentable parents.

A dopey, anthropormorphic dog called Astro. A home where

many rooms existed behind many walls. Nevermind the

obvious— holographic phones, cars that zipped like planes,

robots, meals like vitamins, condensed into a single pill.

 Suspended above earth, there were no trees or birds, sun or

moon, the green of a plush lawn one could step onto from an

open window and track like a thick shag— nothing to indicate

a place of origin; every living scenario stilted and domed,

positioned in the antiseptic serenity of a cirrus-feathered sky.

If this was the future we were watching from the past, then

hands-down I'd trade the present. George never left one night

never to return. June didn't come home some mornings reeking

of smoke and stale booze; beneath her tufted bed-head the

mascara-smudge of Saturn's rings. Judy and Elroy never fought

 over the last sugar sandwich, who was going to steal the next candy bar. Never a parent unavailable to sooth a child sobbing

in bed. Although, at times, the kids complained and the parents

squabbled, the constructed dynamic of their relationships was

always a palliative rinse. And that's why I liked that Hanna-

Barbera show— beneath the obligatory turmoil, their lives

seemed balanced, uncomplicated. Problems that arose didn't

feel "problematic". Merely annoyances, silly insecurities, petty

misunderstandings my brother and I snickered at always

resolved by episode's end.

Copper & Sepia

Shipwrecked hour of old letters. Soot colored cumuli roil
on the horizon, threatening their forecast of wind and rain.
In the agitated froth there are faces I *think* I see, memories
of a distant life transmogrified, scumbled histories
I can recompose. Above is the ashen face of Uncle Ward,
His bedside catheter leaking out the last of his alcoholic
days in the run-down VA. In another formation I see
Holly, our '86 homecoming queen, kinky girl who brandished
my scepter, allowed me to rock the curvature of her back
on the 17th green. To think in the cool dawn, how the chakra
of her dew-ringed body must have glowed. And now, in the
churn and moil of dusk's milky froth, the resemblance of the
first woman who ever *loved* me: Janet Lay, my aunt's ravishing
bridesmade. Her downy features tumble into view.
In the copper and sepia of her correspondence she says
she is committed to the great-redeemer-of-lives.
I imagined there was a wished forgetting, a recurring flaw
in demeanor. At least that's what I read in the tone
of her letters, lengthy epistles that arrived the summer
I turned 14: Olivetti typeface beseeching me to turn my love
unto His side. But her unwavering world proved too much
for me, so I stowed her words in a Converse box
for 30 years. Life of penance, life of proverbs— chaste
world uninviting, unfit for a teenage boy. After all,
I spent time filching condoms, mowing neighbor's grass
for weed, spending whatever trusting heart I could find.
In the foreshortened dusk, every letter ends with the earnest
And simplest of instructions, soulful affectation lost
on me then, underlined and set off with a smiley face.

Crease and powder now held lovingly, then returned
to the white and red cardboard of my youth while out
in the gloaming's fringe I hear the sudden panic of rain.

Marriage: An Unlikely Devotional

I study her face for leads. After all, she's left *me* feeling

ambushed, neutered, like some woebegone lad who's had his

family's coat-of-arms torn down and pissed on in front of

an unsuspecting crowd. A wee o'er the top? Possibly, but, my

good friends, you must understand the dynamics of

the situation. I didn't. And for that there must be a price to pay.

Here it is: my marriage of 22 years and still we go at it, bray at

each other like embittered pack-mules. I pander to her eyes,

gesticulation of hands for incriminating clues. Obviously

there's something I've done or haven't, said or didn't, some

injustice I've caused in my continuity of blind pursuit.

You ask how I know this? Because just ten minutes ago, in this very room where we are surrounded by things we love that

nominally define us— saddle-stitched leather of Italian country,

wedding crystal, vases, sleeping dogs, gesso boards slathered in

acrylics; small trove of originals we sunk money into over

the years— she tells me, point blank, after a long silenc

post-tiff, with steely reserve of the eternally damned, that

"I make things up to impress, to sell a false concern and hope,

that I use my *average* intelligence to distract from those who

regard me most to hide the symptoms of my own narcissistic

condition". She says, " I say things without thinking, that

sometimes, even though I act in-the-know, I haven't

the fucking foggiest clue". In said room, ensconced with said dogs snoozing, freckled with apricot sunspots, I watch

their legs tremble in dream. I imagine the world they run and

leap through in vainglorious joy where they chase-down

visions prey: spooked rabbit, broken-winged bird, cellophane

wrapper cart-wheeling over crimson leaves shed like a lover's

dress in the secret catacombs of night. A FedEx liner rumbles

overhead, spells out the neurotic need for abstraction in its

hieroglyph of jet wash across the champagne sky. And though

there is a palpable, liquefied intensity surging through the air,

I rise without comment, rebuff or spunk rejoinder to seek

palliative rinse of a walk, ambling up nearby trails seeking

restorative of temperate sun and air, leisurely stroll on

meandering switchback which offers nary a clue, credible

insight to bewildering dilemma. Deep in furthest remove,

a trailing cry of gull or loon as I approach a firmly packed

berm, fortress of leaves. I consider its horseshoe shape, open-

ended for mounting or retreat. A small, white flag sunk in its

leveed base. A revenant wind nudges it from a limp. I can't

decide if its emblematic of triumph or defeat.

Upstairs **Hunky Dory** is playing, the orange RCA label
with " Bowie" circling round and round on
the Bang &Olufsen because somebody has decided
to play *Changes*for the umpteenth time. It's the spring
of '86 and my father has left for the East Coast
where a Mapplethorpe exhibit beckons. In his absence,
I render my own art, draw maps of exquisite detail,
each page containing a likeness and notes on location
of his impressive cache of artwork before I have
a U-Haul back up and load it all into temporary storage.
The toga party (alá***Animal House***) was months in the making,
was epic, moviesque, **THE** masterpiece everyone talked about
decades later at class reunions. And while I was sketching
his collection of Mirólithiographs, alabaster statues
and glass tables filled with ancient African tribal masks,
in neighboring bedrooms togas hit the floor,
and on the veranda kind-bud wafted towards the heavens
in thick clouds of particulate smoke, and if you stood
upwind or downwind (whichever the case may be)
you'd experience the verbage of the day: *contact-high,*
until the smokers outside *were* "high" and finally
someone had the good sense to change the vinyl.
But somehow I fucked-up, transposed two of the faces!
Like *Risky Business* the jig was up, " Momma found a crack
in the egg", and mere hours after my father's plane landed
I found myself homeless in the streets of Marion before
I'd even graduated high school. I never returned. Felt like
a Judas all summer. Jesus dunked in a warm jar of piss.

Biographical Note

Tony Tracy's most recent book, *Welcome To Your Life*, is his third collection of poetry (Cybernet.wit). Earlier books of poetry include, The Christening (Center Press, 1997), and Without Notice (March Street Press, 2007). He has published well over 200 poems in journals and magazines nationally, most notably in places like *Tar River Poetry, North American Review, Rattle, Hotel Amerika, Poetry East, Painted Bride Quarterly, Briar Cliff Review, Jelly Bucket, Coe Review, Concho River Review, Slipstream, New Madrid, Poet Lore, Burningword* , and *I-70 Review* to name a few. He lives in Urbandale, Iowa with his wife of nearly 25 years, two sons and two dogs. He enjoys music of all kinds (especially that funkified rock 'n roll), reading in all its vainglory and self-prescribed indulgence, shooting hoops and traveling to the same indiscriminate countries year after year. Some summer days he can be found hanging around the Friendly Confines where he still basks in the waning glow of the Cubs 2016 World Cahmpionship.

www.ingramcontent.com/pod-product-compliance
Lightning Source LLC
LaVergne TN
LVHW041721190726
843493LV00007B/2188